# What is
# WISDOM
## for a
# WOMAN

## Princess Dumebi Grace

*AuthorHouse™*
*1663 Liberty Drive*
*Bloomington, IN 47403*
*www.authorhouse.com*
*Phone: 1 (800) 839-8640*

*Scripture quotations marked KJV are from the Holy Bible, King James Version (Authorized Version). First published*
*in 1611. Quoted from the KJV Classic Reference Bible, Copyright © 1983 by The Zondervan Corporation.*

*Published by AuthorHouse 07/15/2015*

*ISBN: 978-1-5049-2212-8 (sc)*
*ISBN: 978-1-5049-2223-4 (e)*

*Print information available on the last page.*

*Any people depicted in stock imagery provided by Thinkstock are models,*
*and such images are being used for illustrative purposes only.*
*Certain stock imagery © Thinkstock.*

*This book is printed on acid-free paper.*

# The Perfect Little Gift

To

From

# On the occasion of
## (write your personal message)

_____

_____

_____

_____

_____

_____

_____

_____

_____

_____

# ACKNOWLEDGMENTS

All thanks and glory to the Divine Mind, the I AM and everyone who has encouraged me and taught me lessons on this plain called earth. I thank my family, especially my dad, my big brother Anthony, aunty Doris, my sister Lydia and her husband Mudi Akpocha for holding things down for me when I needed them most. I thank my biggest supporter, King Duru, who tells me I can always do better. I thank my friends, Uche Ken, Bash Elliott, April Quiana, Molly, for being there for me. I appreciate you all. My baby,

Celynez, for your patience and understanding with mummy. My maternal uncle Prince Jude Nwoko for your care and support out here in the USA. My salute goes to my big cousin, HRH Charles Anyasi, the King of Idumuje—unor Kingdom, for your support, brotherly advice and words of wisdom. I remember all what you say to me. Thanks to my lawyer, Barr Victor Ogoli for taking care of things for me. My sincere appreciation goes to Erin Cohen, my publishing consultant and the Authorhouse team for making this project come alive in all its beauty and splendor. You guys rock!

Thank you all for your prayers and good energy thoughts towards me. I feel it. I send loving energy back to y'all.
I pray your wishes be fulfilled. THANK YOU.

# DEDICATED TO

Girls, girls, girls

Other mini books in the series

- Wisdom for Riches

- Wicked Wisdom

- Wisdom for Children

- Wisdom Calls Again

*A gracious woman retaineth honour: and strong men retain riches.*

Pro 11:16

Affirmations: I am a woman, I am
a creator, I am honourable.

A woman is a builder and a
bounding force of a family.
Watch your thoughts,
utterances and actions.

Affirmations: I am fearful, I am law, my family is
harmonious. My family is balanced and happy.

*He that troubleth his own house shall inherit the wind: and the fool shall be servant to the wise of heart.*

Pro 11:29

*A virtuous woman is a crown to her husband: but she that maketh ashamed is as rottenness in his bones.*

Pro 12:4

Affirmations: I am in a blissful and loving relationship. I am the pride and crown of my husband and family.

Affirmations: I am a wise woman,

I am grateful that my wishes are

fulfilled daily because my family is
successful, wealthy and blessed and
my children are wise and leaders. My
husband is the head in word, action and in truth.

*Every wise woman buildeth her house: but the foolish plucketh it down with her hands.*

Pro 14:1

*A soft answer turneth away wrath: but grievous words stir up anger.*

Pro 15:1

Affirmations: I am a woman of

wisdom, I am respectful and

respected. My speech is filled with
love and sincerity. My good

intentions are understood whenever I speak. My word is a healer.

Affirmations:


I am an amazing being, I display

divine intelligence, I am fit to be a perfect
wife. I am found by my soul
mate, divine intelligence links me
with my loving and perfect husband. I am
grateful my relation is favoured
with wealth, peace, happiness and love always.

*Whoso findeth a wife findeth
a good thing, and obtaineth
favour of the LORD.*

Pro 18:22

*A foolish son is the calamity of his father: and the contentions of a wife are a continual dropping.*

Pro 19:13

Your complaining has been
compaired to chicken droppings
It smells.

Affirmations: I am intelligent being, I know when to
speak, I am grateful for every blessing I have

especially for the gift of companionship and love. I
am thankful.

Stop nagging and complaining too
much, it destroys your relationship. When People
start to avoid you, check your character.

Affirmations: I exercise restrain and wisdom with
my speech. I am happy and grateful for
the blessing of having a family.

*It is better to dwell in a corner of the housetop, than with a brawling woman in a wide house.*

Pro 21:9

*The mouth of strange women is a deep pit: he that is abhorred of the LORD shall fall therein.*

Pro 22:14

Knowing God is knowing wisdom, the things some women say and do could confuse you to destroy your own house and peace. Avoid fake women.

Affirmations: my female friends are honest and honourable people, I will not be deceive by the lies and fakery of others. I am wise and prudent.

*For a whore is a deep ditch;*
*and a strange woman is a*
*narrow pit.*

Pro 23:27

Take your time to know who a woman is before you open yourself up or invite her into your home. Some people careless about destroying your family.

Affirmations: my intuitions are divine, my associations are refined and a blessing to me and my household.

Stop talking for talking sake, stop judging because
you feel you are better than the other person. Do not say
things to destroy another, except you need to help clarify a
situation or the law requires you to witness against somebody.
Speak only the truth
Affirmations: I am a bearer of the truth, I
behave intelligently, my speeches are to
love, protect and uphold people.

*be not witness against thy neighbor without cause; and deceive not with their lips.*

Prov 24: 28

*say not I will do so to him as he hath done*
*to me; I will render to the man*
*according to his work.*

Prov 24: 29

Life is so much simpler and easier
without revenge. When you are hurt by
someone, forgive and forget which means do not
revenge by so doing you stop the revenge
and hatred cycle. Its victory for you and
mankind because then, no one will want to
revenge on you when you hurt them.

Affirmations: I evolve as a better person, because I
forgive. I dwell in love. Every good to others,
comes back to me. I am wise.

The biggest problems ladies face in a relationship with a man is that of double mindedness which could be defined as unfaithfulness not necessarily sexually cheating. Once you discover that a man is not sure if he wants to be with you, given whatever possible reason to make you feel you aren't good enough. Stay away from such a man. He can be trusted. He will just waste time or years after investing your emotions where you will eventually get hurt but you learn.

Affirmations: I have a partner who loves and cherishes me regardless *confidence in an unfaithful man in time of trouble is like a broken tooth and a foot out of joint.*

Prov 25: 19

Your home is your temple! It should always
be peaceful. Shouting or higher tone of
voice will not solve any problems, it will
only aggravate it. They are other more
peaceful ways and long lasting solutions
to any situation. Find a better, more
classy and lady-like ways to solve issues
Affirmations: I am a woman of honour,
my home is peaceful. I create and atmosphere of love,
abundance and respect for everyone in my home.

*it is better to dwell in the corner of the housetop, than with a brawling woman and in a wide house.*

Prov 25: 24

*it is not good to eat much honey: so for men to search their own glory is not glory.*

Prov 25: 27

Be mindful of what you eat. Avoid eating anything in excess no matter how healthy you feel it is. Moderation in eating should be every woman's watch word. You need to keep that body banging. Even though you know your worth, Avoid self-praise, that's the beginning of failure. Lets others see the good and praise you.

Affirmations: I am aware of the good in me, I act appropriately at all times, my light shines forth at all times.

*he that hath no rule over his own spirit is like a city that is broken down and without walls.*

Prov25: 28

Affirmations:

I have control over my thought because I am infinite, I have a divine mind and I am positive and confident in the ability of infinite intelligence to guide me aright. I am divinely protected.

I have the mind of Christ.

*where no wood is, there the fire goeth out;*
*so where there is no talebearer, strife*
*ceaseth.*

Prov 26: 20

Every problem should be solved without allowing gossips to ruin friendships and family.

Affirmations: I am honest to my friends and family. My circle of friends and relatives are honest and courteous people. I am surrounded by people of love and peace.

I am love.

When you start to praise yourself, pride comes and you begin to feel better than others. Stay humble.

Affirmations: I recognize that we are all equal before The Creator. I am aware that people evolve at different levels and speed. I am thankful for my own level of evolution and awareness. I grow in strength and wisdom daily. I am blessed.

*let another man praise thee, and not thine
own mouth; a stranger, and not thine
own lips*

Prov 27: 2

*open rebuke is better than secret love*

Prov 27: 5,

Affirmations:

I am a woman of wisdom, I show love at all time. I have the mind of Christ, I caution family and loved ones whenever necessary in love and genuine friendship. I

receive wise counsel with open mind.

The society and families tend to focus more on the up bringing of the female child, for her to be the best of herself at all times but forget that the male child must also be taught to assume responsibilities also for their behaviours as it affects the entire society and households. Affirmations: my male children, relatives and friends are all well trained and divinely guided as well as the females in my life. I give thanks for all males in my life, for wisdom to excel.

*correct thy son and he shall give thee rest;*
*yea, he shall give delight unto thy soul.*

prov 29: 17

Spending emotionally and sexually on more than
one woman is giving your manly strength away
Women should train their sons to wait for the
right person and mature emotionally and be
financially independence before getting involved with women.
Ladies should not be involved with a man with
many women.
Affirmation: I am drawn to my soul mate and
real love. We recognize each other with ease.

*give not thy strength unto women, nor thy ways to that which destroyeth kings*

Prov 31: 3

*who can find a virtuous woman? for her*

Prov 31: 10

When there is trust between couples, the man will have no need for another woman to feel more manly. Affirmations: I affirm that I'm truly trusted by my partner and I wholeheartedly trust him too. We are in harmony in thoughts and actions and we manifest greatness individually and collectively as a family.

*the heart of her husband doth safely trust her, so that he shall have no need of spoil.*

v.11

*she will do him good and not evil all the days of her life.*

V.12

If you marry the right partner, you will see mostly positivity and peace in everything you do.

Affirmations:

I am grateful, My union with my partner, my friend, my husband will do us good and bring us greatness daily and forever, we are infinitely and positively aligned.

A perfect woman is willing to work and earn money.
Putting all the responsibility of providing
for the home on the man, is not wise. You both are responsible
for everything. Money, chores, children, peace of the home. Etc.
Affirmations: I am willing and able, I have the
ability to make wealth. I am resourceful. I
am grateful for the strength to earn.

*she seeketh wool, and flax, and worketh willingly with her own hands.*

v.13

Always do you best to get the best for your
family, not minding the cost or distance
you get it from.
Affirmations:
I recognize the best and healthy products
for me and my family, for health
wellness and luxury living. I am grateful
and thankful for the resources available to me.

*she is like the merchants ships; she bringeth her food from afar.*

V.14

*she riseth also while it is yet night and giveth meat to her household, and a portion for her maidens.*

v.15

Always recognize that to be successful, you can't do it all, get assistants and house keepers, train them in love to the standard you want and reward them generously. Take them as your children. Never allow them to take complete charge of your home. Be in charge.

Affirmations: I am articulate and coordinated, I am Happy to provide for my household. Everyone is en sync with routines and activities to help us live a happy and fulfilled life always.

Every woman should own a farm or at least a
garden. It brings so much joy and fulfillment
to plant your food or flowers, watch them grow
and nurture them to maturity. Its an
amazing feeling. You don't have to be the one
tilling the ground if you don't have the time.
You can hire gardeners or farmers.
Affirmations: I love nature, I enjoy nature
and I recognize a good business of farming
for the nourishment of my
family as well as an extra stream of income source.

*she considereth a field, and buyeth it: with the fruit of her hands she planteth a vineyard*

v.16

*she girdeth her loins with strength, and*
*strengtheneth her arms.*

v. 17

There is no room for laziness for a lady. It
is advisable to get adequate rest, but laziness is a no no. be
creative with your thoughts and time. You have endless

possibilities to help your world at the same
time make good money.

Be a strong woman!

Affirmations: I am a woman of strength.

*she perceiveth that her merchandise is good:*
*her candle goeth not out by night.*

v. 18

A good woman never lets anything especially the essentials run out in her home with proper planning. Creating and using the guide of a time table will help eliminate running out of supply. Avoid fake products. Research on products you use.

Affirmations: I am careful, I do not take things for granted, I am grateful for the spirit of perfect coordination and divine wisdom. We have plenty.

Wealth comes through multiple streams of income. It is good to specialize but it is more profitable to have other sources of income streams which should be passive and doesn't require your full time.

Affirmations: I am happy to enjoy multiple streams of income. I share God's ability to multi task and be excellent. I am grateful for the spirit of creative earning.

*she layeth her hands to the spindle, and
her hands hold the distaff.*

v. 19

*she stretcheth out her hands to the
poor; yea, she reacheth forth her
hands to the needy.*

v.20

The primary nature of a woman is love just like GOD. Be willing to give at all times. Open your heart to give and never stop anyone who is willing to give from giving, be also willing to receive.

Affirmations: I am love. Anyone that comes in contact with me feels love and

acceptance. I am always willing to give in love.

A great wife and mother is a great manager,
an excellent home maker.
Affirmations:
I am grateful for the spirit of excellence in
me which is the spirit of Christ, the
transformed soul, more gracious than the
eyes can see. My family is a perfect
example of Gods goodness and care
through care in exhibit in my family.
My life is amazing.

*she is not afraid of the snow for her household: for all her household are clothed in scarlet.*

v. 21

A lady should have class and taste. Fineness should be every woman's watch word.

Affirmations:

I love good things and good things of life naturally flow to me. I am graceful, gracious and classy. My life is adorable.

I am grateful for all God's goodness on me.

*she maketh herself coverings of tapestry;*
*her clothing is silk and purple.*

v. 22

*her husband is known in the gates,*
*when he sitteth among the elders of*
*the land.*

v. 23

When you find a good woman, there is a good
partner around the corner or besides her and vice
versa. If the reverse is the case, prayers
and positive affirmations should be made
in love for the failing partner.

Affirmations: my partner, my husband is
known for goodness and greatness, respect
for family and friends. He is trustworthy and a true lover.

Every virtuous woman, recognizes every opportunity especially business opportunities for herself or her husband.

Affirmations: I am thankful for the opportunities presented before me by divine providence. I recognize and seize the opportunities for my good and the advancement of the human race. Thank you.

*she maketh fine linen, and selleth it;*
*and delivereth girdles unto the merchant.*

v. 24

*strength and honour are her clothing: and she shall rejoice in time to come.*

v. 25

Most times when you begin a project, you
face many obstacles, but you've got to be strong
and believe in the infinite mind to
guide you aright to achieve your set purpose. You also
have to be honourable in your dealings with people.

Affirmations: I am willing and strong enough
to accomplish my goals. I believe the faithfulness
of God to carry me through.

Being kind doesn't mean you should not be
able to discipline, caution and correct
when necessary. You should also be
kind with wisdom. You cant open your
home to every one.
Affirmations:
I am disciplined and kind, I love and speak
in wisdom, I am divine intelligence. I
am grateful the gift of Jesus, the spirit
of wisdom in my life.

*she openeth her mouth with wisdom; and*
*in her tongue is the law of kindness.*

v. 26

*she looketh well to the ways of her household, and eateth not the bread of idleness.*

v. 27

If you want to have idle time as a woman, spend
that time with a child, or some other person's
child who is probably not always around or a relative in
conversation to impart some of your wisdom and encouragement
to that person. Create alone time for meditation and listening
to music and things that will keep your spirit happy.


Affirmations: I am efficient and I am involved
in beneficial activities always. I am happy My
home is well taken care of always.

*her children arise up, and call her blessed; her husband also, and he praiseth her.*

v. 28

A good woman cannot breed disrespectful children and home staff, because they have learnt by the example of their mother or the woman in their life. Even the man in her life will readjust his position if he finds a respectful woman.

Affirmations:

I am a blessing to my children and everyone. I am a treasure and a blessing to my husband, they find peace and harmony always

They are beautiful and wonderful women all
around but there is always a distinguishing factor. A woman
who loves, goes after peace always, honours her spouse,
respects herself and others and has excellent work ethics and
believes in the infinite, the divine mind is far above all other.
Affirmations: I am privileged to feel love and be
loved, I am grateful for all Gods blessings. I am
humbled by immeasurable provisions of
great friends and family and resources. I am
overwhelmed by goodness. I am thankful.

*many daughters have done virtuously,*
*but thou excelletst them all.*

v. 29

No matter what you have on this earth, beauty...wealth etc, know the SOURCE, of our being and acknowledge the divine in everything, it is the knowledge we have come to gain here. No matter how far we have come, we recognize that we are more than this earth, we are not alone. That is your crown of glory. we are source energy.

Affirmation: I am that I am.

*Favour is deceitful, and beauty is vain:*
*but a woman that feareth the Lord,*
*she shall be praised.*

v. 30

*give her of the fruit of her hands; and let her own works praise her in the gates.*

v. 31

We are co-creators on this earth, so we create our own space, our realities. Everything we have created with our imaginations and our own hands (action), we will definitely enjoy it here on earth

Affirmations: I am aware of the powers bestowed
on me to create what I want, I am
grateful for the choices I have made. I choose to
live happy and abundant, I choose to have
happy and fruitful people around me. I choose
to enjoy this life.

# Addendum

I used to call myself a simple girl until I saw a verse of the bible that says so boldly "woe to the simple". I was to say the least stunned at my new discovery, I set out to understand what it means for me as a girl not to be just simple. There has to be an opposite of being simple which I eventually found out to be wisdom. What is then wisdom for a woman?

"What is then wisdom for a woman?".

To learn wisdom watch people around us to learn from them, learn from our own mistakes and most importantly we always have to go back to history.

It is said that king Solomon was the wisest
king that ever live and he was also very vast

In the affairs of women, married 700 women
and had 300 concubines, in modern terminology, they
would be called mistresses or girlfriends.

The instructions and wise counsels or advice in the
book of proverbs cannot be over emphasized.

This book show a woman how to live from
proverbs point of view. How to deal with
situations, to make sure you earn money.

Many or some ladies want to wait for a man
to come and provide for her, in this foregoing passages, this is
not advisable, to command self respect, a woman must work and

earn, be kind and loving as well as be respectful of others especially your spouse. Respect begets respect, so if you respect others, you will in turn be respected. This is not encouraging any lady to accept abuse from anyone or because you earn money,

You should accept a man who is not earning or putting enough effort and faith to earn just as you do. Do not accept what you don't want. A virtuous woman has to have a man who is also virtuous, people know him as a good man. The children of a wise woman are also wise, they exhibit, self respect, love intelligence and are excellent examples to their peers. A wise woman cannot live any stone unturned. Every aspect of her life

Must be properly taken care of. Delegate
whenever necessary, treat staff with respect,
they are not slaves, they are with you
to help in attaining your higher self just as
they also want to attain their higher selves.

Everything you want has to be created by
you, as it is said, time is an illusion, your age
doesn't make any difference in getting whatever
you want, as soon as you find wisdom,

Run with wisdom, wisdom to be an excellent
partner or wife, wisdom to be an excellent mother if
you choose to have children, wisdom to be an excellent

friend and relative, wisdom to be an entrepreneur or a
business woman. Wisdom to take care of your female
body to look good always, being sexy as
woman is your emotional gift of pleasure to
your husband and to yourself. Get wisdom to find your
higher self, to be truly beautiful inside and outside.

Wisdom is the principal thing, find your higher self is finding
God, this is what brings you all the praises you aspire for.
Finding yourself, your purpose, finding God in YOU. This is the
wisdom of all wisdom. Then you can create
your world as you so want it.

Live beautiful! Live wise! God speed.

Other mini books in the series

- wisdom calls again

- Wisdom for riches

- Wicked wisdom

- Wisdom for children

# Notes

# Notes

# Notes

Printed in the United States
By Bookmasters